Mammal Mania

Debra J. Housel

Consultants

Timothy Rasinski, Ph.D.
Kent State University
Bill Houska, D.V.M.
James K. Morrisey, D.V.M.

Publishing Credits

Dona Herweck Rice, *Editor-in-Chief*
Robin Erickson, *Production Director*
Lee Aucoin, *Creative Director*
Conni Medina, M.A.Ed., *Editorial Director*
Jamey Acosta, *Editor*
Heidi Kellenberger, *Editor*
Lexa Hoang, *Designer*
Lesley Palmer, *Designer*
Stephanie Reid, *Photo Editor*
Rachelle Cracchiolo, M.S.Ed., *Publisher*

Image Credits
Cover haveseen/Shutterstock; p.3 Matej Hudovernik/Shutterstock; p.4-5 Arsgera/Shutterstock; p.4 Ammit/Shutterstock; p.5 Xavier Marchant/Shutterstock; p.6-7 val lawless/Shutterstock; p.6 Stefan Petru Andronache/Shutterstock; p.7 Karel Gallas/Shutterstock; p.8-9 Anan Kaewkhammul/Shutterstock; p.8 Brett Atkins/Shutterstock; p.9 top to bottom: oksana.perkins/Shutterstock; Studio 37/Shutterstock; p.10-11 Sean Gladwell/Shutterstock; p.10 Nagel Photography/Shutterstock; p.11 top to bottom: xstockerx/Shutterstock; Eric Isselée/Shutterstock; tezzstock/Shutterstock; Albie Venter/Shutterstock; p.12 Kjersti Joergensen/Shutterstock; p.13 Kjersti Joergensen/Shutterstock; p.13 Mogens Trolle/Shutterstock; p.14-15 Darklight/Shutterstock; p.14 top to bottom: p.14 palko72/Shutterstock; Zerli/Dreamstime; Vladimir Chernyanskiy/Shutterstock; p.15 M.Shcherbyna/Shutterstock; Sergey Rusakov/Shutterstock; p.16-17 shooarts/Shutterstock; p.16 top to bottom: Kirsanov/Shutterstock; John Carnemolla/Shutterstock; p.17 top to bottom: NHPA/ZUMA Press/Newscom; ZSSD/Minden Pictures; p.18-19 val lawless/Shutterstock; p.18 CraigRJDCraigRJD/istockphoto; p.19 Jiri Haureljuk/Shutterstock; p.20-21 Michal Ninger/Shutterstock; p.20 clearviewstock/Shutterstock; p.21 Dave Watts/Alamy; p.21 Michal Ninger/Shutterstoc; p.22-23 Sean Gladwell/Shutterstock; p.22 top to bottom: Eric Isselée/Shutterstock; p.23 left to right: Christian Musat/Shutterstock; neelsky/Shutterstock; Andreka/Shuttertsock; p.24-25 VVO/Shutterstock; p.24 top to bottom: 33karen33/iStockphoto; Steshkin Yevgeniy/Shutterstock; p.25 James Simon/Photo Researchers, Inc.; p.26-27 Darklight/Shutterstock; p.26 top to bottom: Natali Glado/Shutterstock; haveseen/Shutterstock; p.27 Darklight/Shutterstock; p.28 Arsgera/Shutterstock; background: Nadezhda Bolotina/Shutterstock; Lukiyanova Natalia/frenta/Shutterstock; back cover: Stefan Petru Andronache/Shutterstock

Based on writing from *TIME For Kids*.

Teacher Created Materials

5301 Oceanus Drive
Huntington Beach, CA 92649-1030
http://www.tcmpub.com
ISBN 978-1-4333-3658-4
© 2012 Teacher Created Materials, Inc.
Printed in China
Nordica.012019.CA21801581

Table of Contents

What Is a Mammal?

They come in many shapes and sizes. They may swim in oceans or run through deserts and fields. Some climb trees or cliffs. They live in rainforests, frozen places, and even in your home. What are they? Mammals!

jaguar

orca (killer whale)

There is at least one mammal living in your home. You! Humans are mammals.

A rabbit's body stays 102°F at all times. ➤

Mammals are warm-blooded animals. They are called **vertebrates** (VUR-tuh-breyts) because they have backbones.

rabbit

Being warm-blooded means that a mammal's body stays the same **temperature** at all times. In order to do this, a mammal must eat lots of food. It also has hair, fur, or a layer of fat to keep it warm. Sometimes it has more than one of these. A polar bear has both thick fur and fat because it is always cold where it lives.

Did you know that being in water cools your body? You get cold if you stay in too long. Since water mammals spend their lives in the water, they have a layer of fat to **insulate** (IN-suh-leyt) their bodies. It holds in their warmth.

seal

Food = Energy

Mammals eat a lot of food in order to make energy. The energy keeps them warm.

▲ Fat and fur keep seals warm by protecting them from the cold, just as a thick coat helps you stay warm.

humpback whale

Some mammals, like whales, live in the sea. Others live on land. Land mammals have four **limbs**. No matter where they live, all mammals breathe with lungs.

Limbs

A land mammal's limbs are its legs and arms.

All water mammals must come to the surface to breathe.

dolphins

9

Offspring

The offspring of an animal are its babies. Babies come from, or "spring off," their parents.

baby pigs

Male and female mammals must mate in order to have **offspring**. Most mammal babies grow inside their mothers. The mothers give birth to live **young**. The young are born helpless, so they need a parent's care. They must drink their mothers' milk. It may take weeks or years before they can take care of themselves. Just think of how long it will take you to grow up!

The time a mother carries her babies before giving birth is called **gestation** (je-STEY-shuhn). The number of days is different for each **species** (SPEE-sheez).

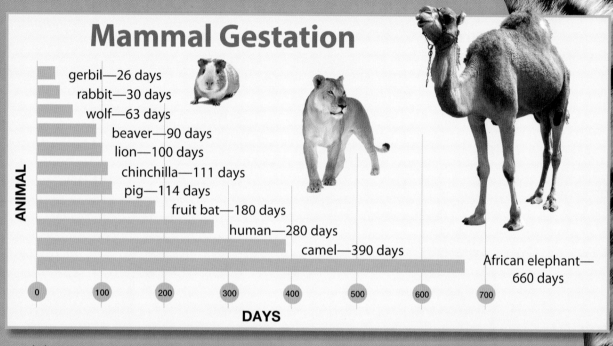

Mammal Gestation

gerbil—26 days
rabbit—30 days
wolf—63 days
beaver—90 days
lion—100 days
chinchilla—111 days
pig—114 days
fruit bat—180 days
human—280 days
camel—390 days
African elephant—660 days

ANIMAL

0   100   200   300   400   500   600   700

DAYS

▼ Mother cheetahs move their cubs to a new hiding place every few days.

Did You Know?

A species is an animal group such as cats, dogs, rabbits, or bears. A species can also be a plant group such as roses, daisies, or pine trees.

cheetahs

Kinds of Mammals

Scientists group mammals by the things they have in common. One group, **primates**, is the species name for humans, apes, and monkeys.

Most primates have thumbs. Thumbs let primates grab and pick up things. Most primates are **omnivores** (OM-nuh-vohrs) because they can eat both plants and animals.

mother and baby orangutan

macaque monkey

A lioness ➤
hunts a zebra.

Wolves, lions, and otters are all **carnivores** (KAHR-nuh-vohrs). They eat only meat. Carnivores are **predators** (PRED-uh-ters). They hunt and catch **prey**.

How are deer, giraffes, and cows alike? They have hooves. Hoofed mammals are **herbivores** (HUR-buh-vohrs), which means they eat only plants. The larger the animal, the more plants it must eat.

donkey hoof

▲ A giraffe's long neck has seven vertebrae. That's the same number that humans have!

beaver

▲ Chewing wood keeps a
beaver's teeth from
growing too long.

Rodents

Some rodents, such as chipmunks,
eat only plants. They are herbivores.
Others, such as rats, eat meat and
plants. They are omnivores.

Most mammals have jaws and teeth. **Rodents**
and rabbits have front teeth that grow constantly.
They must chew hard things like tree bark to keep
their teeth from becoming too long.

Do you have a pet rodent? You do if you have a
mouse, a gerbil, or a hamster.

Odd Mammals

Odd mammals are different from all others. For example, anteaters have no teeth. Instead, they have long **snouts** and catch bugs with their sticky tongues. They swallow bugs whole.

All mammals can move. People walk, bears climb, kangaroos jump, and whales swim. But only one mammal can fly. It's a bat!

▼ There are about 1,000 different kinds of bats.

Not Really Flying

Flying squirrels may look as if they could fly, but they can't. They just control how they fall by gliding. Flying squirrels glide from tree to tree to find food. Sometimes they glide as far as 295 feet to reach a new tree.

flying squirrel

An anteater's tongue can be up to two feet long. ➤

Marsupials (mahr-SOO-pee-uhls) are another group of odd mammals. They give birth to babies that are alive but not ready to survive apart from their mothers.

Each baby must live for weeks or months in its mother's pouch. Many marsupials, including the kangaroo, live in Australia.

tree kangaroo

▲ A marsupial baby stays in its mother's pouch.

eastern gray kangaroo

Australia and a few nearby islands are home to the strangest mammals of all. They are called **monotremes** (MON-uh-treems). What makes them so strange? They lay eggs!

Why Are They Mammals?

Monotremes are called mammals because they provide milk for their young.

echidna

platypus

The platypus (PLAT-i-pus) lays its eggs in a nest. After ten days the babies hatch. The mother lies on her back. The babies lick up the milk that oozes from a gland on the surface of her belly. Her milk flows for about two months.

The other mammal that lays eggs is the echidna (ih-KID-nuh).

Life Spans and Habitats

Different mammals can live for different lengths of time. This graph shows the number of years each kind of animal normally lives. Most members of the species die by the age given. A few live longer.

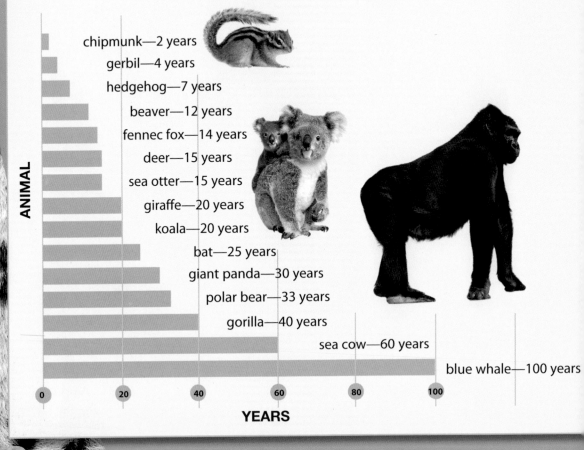

Mammal Life Spans

chipmunk—2 years
gerbil—4 years
hedgehog—7 years
beaver—12 years
fennec fox—14 years
deer—15 years
sea otter—15 years
giraffe—20 years
koala—20 years
bat—25 years
giant panda—30 years
polar bear—33 years
gorilla—40 years
sea cow—60 years
blue whale—100 years

ANIMAL

0   20   40   60   80   100

YEARS

Mammals live in **habitats** all over the world. Because they are warm-blooded, their bodies stay the right temperature no matter where they live. Some mammals live in deserts while others live in a snowy wilderness. How can this be? Each mammal has body features **suited** to where it lives.

The fennec fox and the camel live in the desert. Both can live for days without drinking water. The fennec fox's large ears let extra heat leave its body to keep it from getting too hot.

The musk ox and the Arctic hare live where it gets very cold in the winter. It never gets hot there, even in the summer. They have heavy fur to protect them from the cold.

fennec fox

musk ox

Monkeys live in rain forests where it's always hot and **humid**. Chinchillas live on mountains. Whales live in saltwater. Some sea cows live in freshwater. You can find mammals almost everywhere!

sea cow

◄ A chinchilla's thick fur lets it live high on cold mountains.

Some mammals hibernate during the winter.

ground squirrel

Some mammals live where there are big changes between the seasons. These animals must survive the heat of summer. They must also survive the bitter cold of winter. Many animals spend the winters **hibernating**.

During the warm months, these animals eat all the food they can find. This builds a layer of fat on their bodies. When it gets cold, they go into a cave or a hole in the ground. They fall asleep, and their heart and lungs slow down. They look dead, but they're just asleep. Their bodies live on their stored fat. When spring comes, they awaken.

Desert rats do something similar, except they sleep during the hottest, driest season. Then, they are active during the cooler times of the year. Sleeping during the summer is called **aestivation** (es-tuh-VEY-shun).

As you can see, mammals are very interesting creatures. Aren't you glad to be one?

red panda

tarsier monkey

Glossary

aestivation—to rest during hot and dry conditions

carnivores—animals that eat only meat

gestation—the amount of time a mammal spends developing inside its mother

habitats—the places where animals live

herbivores—animals that eat only plants

hibernating—spending the winter in a resting state

humid—moist

insulate—to keep heat from escaping

limbs—the body parts that stick out from an animal's main body, such as arms and legs

marsupials—mammals that carry their young in a pouch

monotremes—mammals that lay eggs

odd—unusual or strange

offspring—the young of an animal or plant

omnivores—animals that eat both plants and meat

predators—animals that hunt, kill, and eat other animals

prey—animals that are hunted, killed, and eaten by other animals

primates—the group of mammals that have hands (usually with thumbs) instead of paws

rodents—a group of mammals with four limbs and sharp front teeth that grow all the time

snouts— especially long noses

species—a group of animals or plants that are like each other

suited—fitting or made for

temperature—an amount of heat measured by a thermometer

vertebrates—animals that have spines (backbones)

young—babies; animals before they become adults

Index